HOW TO BE SUCCESSFUL AT THE VIRGINIA MILITARY INSTITUTE

HOW TO BE SUCCESSFUL AT THE VIRGINIA MILITARY INSTITUTE

THE KEYS TO SUCCESS WRITTEN BY A CADET FOR FUTURE CADETS

COLIN D. SMITH '19

© 2019 Colin D. Smith

All rights reserved. This book or any portion thereof may not be reproduced or used in any manner whatsoever without express written permission.

ISBN: 978-1-09-624285-7

*For Sean Duc Hoang,
the first member of the VMI Class of 2019*

Table of Contents

Introduction 1
Mentality 5
Time Management 9
Organization 13
Academics 15
Physical Fitness 21
Nutrition 27
Sleep 31
Leadership 35
Finding the Balance 41
Acknowledgments 43

Introduction

My name is Colin Smith, and at the time of composing this guide, I was a first classman (senior) at VMI in the Class of 2019. While I'm by no means the most successful person to go through the school, or even in my class, I have narrowed down what has made me successful and identified the most significant things that I wish someone had taught me prior to my matriculation in 2015. These things led me to earn a great GPA during my rat year, crush my fitness goals, and stay mentally healthy throughout my cadetship. As a result, I am one step closer to accomplishing my goal of becoming an Army dentist, and will be attending VCU's School of Dentistry on the Army HPSP scholarship. Whether you're about to matriculate for your first fall semester at VMI, a current cadet trying to get his/her life together, or simply considering VMI as a college option, this guide's intent is to provide insight into how not only to survive but excel at a tough and unique military college.

I want to start off by telling a short story. One of the greatest events at VMI is without a doubt the VMI Ring Figure. At this event, second classmen (juniors) receive their VMI rings. The VMI ring represents everything that a class has endured throughout their time at VMI. Just like any other second classman, I got my ring in November and was very excited about it. The following semester we had our Spring concert, an event where everyone can eat good food, drink beer (if 21+), and listen to whatever artist the school invited to perform. Approximately thirty of my BR's (brother rats) and I decided to have a cookout before the concert at the Maury River. After some drinks and a lot of fun, I decided to skip some rocks on the river. On one of my last attempts, I noticed that there were two splashes in the water. What the heck? Then it hit me. One splash was from the rock I threw and the other was from my VMI ring. The ring that I had just gotten the previous semester, and the ring that I had drained my entire bank account in order to purchase. My stomach was in a knot. I stood there, dumbfounded by what I had just done. One of my BR's noticed me staring into the water and asked what had happened. Before I knew it, about twenty BR's were in the water with their pants rolled up trying to pan for my ring under water.

About twenty-five minutes passed and still no luck. I decided to call off the search. How could I have been so careless? One of my more inebriated BR's came up to me and said something like, "Colin, I heard you lost your ring. Let me look for it." I rolled my eyes and reluctantly pointed to the general area of where I think it entered the water. He jumped in and after searching for a bit, apologized and said it must be lost. Before leaving for the concert, he said, "Hey Colin, looking for this?" He held up my ring, covered in mud, on his middle finger and started laughing. I couldn't believe my eyes. What were the odds that he could reach down into the mud and pull out my ring after so much time had passed?

I love telling this story because it serves as a great example of how VMI works. When you're at your lowest point and feel like there's no hope at all, your BR's will surprise you and go to extreme lengths to get you back on track. If you learn nothing from this guide, I want you to remember that the comradery at VMI isn't just an admissions tactic. You will benefit the most from the Institute by working together and having each other's back. Don't be afraid to seek out help and offer help to those in need. So without further ado, let's get started.

Mentality

The hardest part about attending VMI is not what you would naturally guess: academics, fitness, military training, etc. Instead, I would argue that the level of difficulty you come up against is dependent on one thing: your mentality. The ratline is a mental game. You'll hear over and over that you just have to figure it out as you go along, but I'm here to tell you that even though a lot of your growth and learning will stem from direct experiences, there are definitely things you can pick up even before coming to VMI that will play into your success.

So what should my mentality be? The hardest thing to accept is that you aren't the only one struggling. You have to realize that the system is designed to "break people down" and challenge them to their core. It's easy to acquire the mindset that you have it harder than everyone else and that you are being treated differently. However, that's the ultimate beauty of the system. The best way to grow is to be placed in a state of discomfort. Only from there can you adjust your habits and mentality in order to conform to the expectations of VMI. On top of that, people have this notion that the stress and hardship ends when the ratline is over. Get rid of that thought immediately. The ratline helps you develop good habits and develop comradery with your brother rats. After the ratline, it's easy to fall back into old ways. It's easy to become lazy. You suddenly feel like you have more time on your hands than ever. You start procrastinating, putting off your work until the last minute. "Oh, I wrote a 5-page essay during the ratline and it only took me a few hours." You keep telling yourself these things, justifying your complacency, until suddenly it's the night before and you haven't even started the essay.

As a chemistry major, I was taught that entropy is the driving force of the universe. In simple terms, entropy is the favorability of things to become disordered. Yep, that's right, the driving force of the universe is disorder. Here's a classic example: Let's say you clean your room and make it spotless for a VMI room inspection. Before you know it, all that hard work you put in to make your room clean is gone. You have clothes on the back of your chair, your desk isn't organized, maybe your papers are all over the place. Once again, you have to exert more energy just to reach that same state of cleanliness. Surprisingly, it didn't take much energy or effort at all for it to become disordered. What can we learn from this simple, yet inciteful example? In order to be successful, we need to constantly combat entropy, or more simply, resist disorder. The more time you let the universe become disordered, the greater energy will be required to get it back to where you want it. Therefore, going back to my example, it's much easier to exert the small energy required to clean up a few disordered things the day after the inspection than it is to wait an entire week (or for some cadets, until the next inspection) to clean up a mess that requires a ton of energy.

As you can see, we can use our knowledge of this concept to our advantage and apply it to everything we do at VMI. In other words, if you have the mentality: "I am going to do this now because it will cost me less energy," then you will be a step ahead of most of your peers at VMI. Combine this mentality with the realization that you aren't the only one struggling and you'll be well on your way to being a successful rat/cadet.

Lastly, you need to realize that your cadre isn't personally "attacking" you. You will get yelled at. Everyone does. It's easy to start believing they hate you, or at least that they think you don't belong at VMI. If you're hard on yourself already, then you will really struggle with this situation in the ratline. I was a Hotel Company Cadre Corporal and Master Sergeant. Believe me when I say that your cadre doesn't actually think those things about you. After cadre time, most of them go back to their room and nap and don't even think about you until the next cadre time. It's their job to put you under pressure and test your mental fortitude. Don't spend the rest of your day or week stressing over what they said to you at the last cadre time. They've already forgotten about it. Brush it off and keep putting forward maximum effort.

Time Management

If I had to choose one tool that VMI has presented me that has contributed towards my success, it would be time management. Notice how I worded that phrase: "that VMI has presented me...." Many people enter VMI with the idea that the school will give them everything they need to be successful, that you're forced to develop good habits and you have no choice but to stick with them. This is far from the truth. VMI presents or offers good habits to rats/cadets, and it is up to the individual to take advantage of them and reap their benefits. Just because you have 20 credits and a bunch of leadership duties on top of that, doesn't mean you are going to be forced to carve out sufficient time for all of it.

So, what's the secret? You have to do two things. The first step is to develop a written schedule. This sounds like common sense, but you would be surprised how many people neglect such a valuable exercise. It's one of those tedious exercises that people will do for a week or two and then suddenly stop doing it. Why? Entropy. It's easier to be disordered. It takes energy to sit down and plan out your entire week, and many people think that they could be spending that time getting ahead on their tasks for the week instead. But with no guidance or strict schedule to keep you focused during the week, how can you manage your time wisely with the stress and exhaustion that may be clouding your judgment? You probably can't.

What I have found most effective over the past four years at VMI is to use Sunday night as my "planning night" for that week. I start by filling in the time slots in which I have mandatory duties, or things that I absolutely cannot miss (classes, formations, inspections, meetings, lunch, etc.). After that, I make a list on the side that contains everything I want to accomplish that week (three workouts, keeping my room clean, the first three paragraphs of my English essay due the following week, studying for a chemistry test on Friday). This is where the second step comes into play: be reasonable. When filling in your open time slots with these tasks for the week, you have to consider how you will be feeling during those specific times. For example, if I know that I'm exhausted after my back-to-back classes from 0800-0950 on Wednesdays, I'm not going to schedule a chemistry study session from 1000-1200. I won't retain much of the information and I won't be motivated to learn. Instead, I might schedule some studying from 1100-1200 and do my second hour of studying from 2000-2100 in the evening. If I can apply that same logic for studying chemistry on two or three more days of the week, then I will go into Friday's test with six to eight hours of studying under my belt. Additionally, if you write out your schedule and find that you have to sacrifice sleep or eating a meal in order to accomplish everything or if you are left with no time to relax each day, then you need to reduce your list using your priorities. Generally, my priorities look like this:

academics > organization > fitness

VMI has mandatory physical training time on Mondays and Fridays, so cutting out one of those three workouts and replacing it with studying isn't a huge deal. Also, your priorities might vary each week. If you're happy with the way your classes are going, make organization and fitness your priority that week.

After making my schedule for the week, I find it useful to write each day's tasks along with its time on a small notecard and keep it in my cover (hat). I cannot stress how important time management will be in your cadetship. If you stay realistic in your scheduling and prioritize your goals for each week, then you will find that you are able to accomplish much more in the long run.

Organization

Now that you've learned about managing your time wisely at VMI via a written schedule, it's time to discuss overall organization. Organization is important for mental clarity so that you can effectively execute your plans for the week. There's nothing worse than starting your day by getting out of your hay and seeing your wall locker in shambles. This automatically produces stress inside of you and all sense of motivation vanishes. On top of that, you aren't inclined to sit down at your desk to do some work if the papers you need are lost in an intimidating mixture of papers from every class. This was a difficult thing for me to learn, since I am inherently a messy person (my mom will agree).

This is where my written schedule really helped. I started incorporating cleaning into my routine. Every night before I go to bed, I like to pick up my area to make sure that my papers are organized by class, my wall locker is in order, and that my brass and uniform are looking good for the next day. After implementing this routine, I noticed that I woke up in a much better mood and that I was more inclined to complete my tasks throughout the day.

As an incoming rat, you will learn exactly how your room and uniform needs to look at all times, but it's up to you on how you are going to make sure that happens every day. If you're a current cadet and struggling with it, then I promise cleaning for twenty minutes before bed every night will make this worry completely disappear. Make it a habit and stick to it, and watch your entire mentality improve.

Academics

Perhaps the biggest worry for some people coming to VMI is academics. Maybe high school was easy for you and you managed to spend an hour or two of studying the night before a test and still got an A. Well, welcome to college. If you truly wish to be successful, the "night before" technique is not going to fly anymore. There are more assignments, harder assignments, and what feels like less time to complete them all. The key to conquering it is by spreading out your studying. Not only does this reduce your stress levels by allowing you to get more sleep, but it also serves as a more effective study habit. The best way to remember something is through repetition. Therefore, by having smaller study sessions throughout the week, you are reinforcing that knowledge in your brain. You are also more likely to stay motivated using this method. When I used to study the night before, I would stay up until 0300 and just try to cram as much knowledge as possible into my head in the shortest amount of time. When taking the test the next morning, my head felt cloudy and I would confuse a lot of information. After switching to the study habit of an hour here and there throughout the week, I could get sufficient sleep the night before and the information was much easier to recall when taking the test. Even if you get good grades studying the night before, the side effects that accompany lack of sleep will render you almost ineffective the following day. In your head, you crushed that test. Yet, you can't figure out why you're so lazy and have to skip your workout the next day.

Another piece of advice you will receive before matriculation is that "you have to get out of barracks to study." This holds true throughout your entire cadetship. The way our rooms are structured and the close proximity to distractions (loud roommates, tempting video games, your comfy looking hay), it is better just to eliminate these things by leaving barracks. By putting on a uniform and placing yourself in an environment that is solely meant for learning, you are completely committing yourself to being focused and accomplishing tasks. I would recommend checking out the bottom floor of Preston Library or trying to find an empty classroom in one of the academic buildings. Eventually, you'll find a location that works for you and it will become your "go-to study spot."

Once you are in an environment conducive to learning, you have to realize that you must cater your study technique to the class for which you are studying. A big problem I see a lot of college kids struggling with is that they use one technique for every single class. While studying by making a quizlet and writing out the answers to possible essay prompts may work for history, you have to realize that the same thing probably won't work for biology. Maybe for that class drawing out diagrams and annotating the book would work better. Switch it up and see what works.

I also want to cover something that I like to call "academic endurance." What do I mean? Transitioning into VMI as a straight-A student in high school, I set my personal expectations extremely high. This was going to be my big 4.0 moment—I was going to get into every graduate school I applied to, be the best mechanical engineering major at the school, get recognized for a groundbreaking research publication...blah blah blah. Fast forward to the present, I am now a chemistry major that didn't get into every graduate school, and I don't have any research publications. The reason I'm telling you this is because I don't want you to do what I did. A lot can change throughout your cadetship and it's much better to come in with an open mind and explore the different opportunities. If you do come in with the mindset that I had, then the first bad test grade will be crushing. This is where "academic endurance" comes into play. It's easy to let that one poor grade defeat you and ruin the way you view that course for the rest of the semester. What's the point in working hard in this class if I'm just going to get low grades? You might argue that you would never have that mentality. Well, let me paint a picture.

Let's say that I study a few hours every day in preparation for a big test at the end of the week. In addition, I decide to neglect two of my workouts that week just to make sure I'm extra-prepared. My motivation is high and I've been doing really well in the ratline. The day of the test I accidentally sleep through my alarm and my cadre is all over me about it. Not only that, but I forget to pack my calculator while scrambling to get ready that morning. So I sprint back to my room to grab it, and when I finally get to the classroom the test has already started. Now I'm out of breath, stressed out, and to put icing on the cake, the test mainly consists of concepts that I thought wouldn't be very important. The professor grades them that same day, and as I'm getting ready for bed I see that I bombed the test. Do you think you'd be able to study for the next test with the same motivation and optimism as the last? I doubt it.

So what can be done? After feeling sorry for myself and letting a couple bad grades defeat me, I realized that the best thing to do is set up a meeting with my professor to go over the test. You need to go into that meeting prepared to explain your frustration. I remember being visibly frustrated going into a meeting with one of my professors and they realized how I was feeling and calmed me down. They showed me a breakdown of their grading system and I realized that I wasn't as doomed as I thought. Not only does meeting with your professor show them that you care about your grade, but also that you're willing to make any changes necessary to succeed in their course. Many rats/cadets don't realize that their professors are willing to do everything they can to help them succeed. At other schools, this might not be the case with much larger lectures, containing hundreds of students. We have an advantage, so capitalize on it.

Lastly, I want to cover the long-term. You can start setting yourself up for academic success as early as rat year. Luckily, I didn't have to figure this out the hard way and made time to sit down with my academic advisor at the very beginning. Ask them to help you make a plan for when you are going to take each course throughout your cadetship. This removes the possibility of being surprised when you have a "heavier-than-normal" semester, or worst case, getting to first class year and realizing you didn't take some of the required courses. Since rat year consists of a lot of adjustments and stress, most people, including me, take a much lighter load the first semester. I would recommend aiming for 16 credits or below. This allows you to obtain an idea of what kind of college student you are and provides an opportunity to play with your schedule and experiment with different study techniques. Keep in mind that the first semester ultimately sets the tone for the rest of your cadetship. If you start off with a terrible GPA, your entire cadetship will be spent trying to recover and just the thought of academics will get you down and crush motivation. If a cadet is reading this and you are among those that are trying to salvage their GPA, you have to stay positive. Going back to the idea of "academic endurance," you'd be wise to meet with your professors as often as possible, fostering an intrinsic desire to improve. Once again, it all comes back to your mindset, time management, and organization.

VMI HONOR CODE

"A Cadet will not lie, cheat, steal, nor tolerate those who do"

The VMI Honor System is another unique aspect of the Institute. Don't worry though, there will be plenty of training throughout Hell Week that will quickly bring you up to speed. The Honor System isn't something to fear, it's something to be proud of. Without it, your VMI diploma wouldn't mean nearly as much after graduation. Companies and military branches know that they are adding a trustworthy individual to their organization when they see you graduated from VMI.

Physical Fitness

Maybe your biggest worry is the physical fitness aspect at VMI, or maybe you consider yourself fit already and you just want to ensure that you're prepared upon arrival. The first fitness test you will take at VMI is the VFT (VMI Fitness Test). As a rat, you will take your first one during Hell Week, which will serve as a baseline to assess your initial fitness abilities. The test consists of three events in this order: pull-ups (overhand—often confused with a chin-up), two minutes of sit-ups, and a timed 1.5-mile run. This is the part of the guide that could get really controversial, because it seems like everyone at VMI has strict beliefs when it comes to training in the gym. For this reason, I'm only going to cover exercises and mention programs that I have personally completed and have experienced improvement from. I am in no way claiming to be an expert, but merely informing you through my direct experiences. Below is a chart that contains exercises or programs that will help you pass each event, and when done in conjunction with one another, should help you crush that first PT test during Hell Week.

Event:	Pull-ups (No time limit)	Sit-ups (Max in 2 min.)	1.5-mile run (Timed)
Exercise if below the minimum score:	1. Pull-up negatives 2. Assisted pull-ups (bands or machine) 3. Lat pulldowns	1. Max sets of crunches 2. Flutter kicks 3. Leg raises	1. Start with 3 days a week where you run 2 miles (don't worry about speed). 2. Work up to 3 days a week where you run 3 miles (again, speed doesn't matter yet). 3. Finally, run your hardest 3 days a week for 1-mile and time yourself.

Exercise if below the maximum score:	1. Armstrong pull-up program 2. Static holds with chin above the bar for time 3. Lat pulldowns 4. Grip endurance work—sets of max "hang time," or other grip training found on the internet. 5. "Hard to Kill Fitness Programs by Tim Kennedy"	1. Max sets of sit-ups, Hanging leg raises 2. Weighted Russian twists 3. "Hard to Kill Fitness Programs by Tim Kennedy"	1. Incorporate 400m sprints into your current running program with a small rest in between each one. Aim for 8 sets. 2. Another option is to run 200m sprints at the same pace as your goal run time. Aim for 10-12 of these. 3. I also like to train for a 2-mile distance sometimes (tricks your mind into thinking 1.5-miles isn't that bad).
Exercise if above the maximum score:	1. Weighted pull-ups 2. Weighted static holds with chin above the bar for time 3. "Hard to Kill Fitness Programs by Tim Kennedy"	1. Max sets of hanging leg raises 2. Hanging static holds with weight added on top of thighs 3. Weighted sit-ups 4. "Hard to Kill Fitness Programs by Tim Kennedy"	1. Personally, I would just maintain at this point. 2. But if you're dead-set on improving more, I would do large sets of sprints at the pace of your goal run-time.

Again, this is a list of different exercises that I wish I had known about when training for VMI or even just earlier in my cadetship. Most of my improvement came from Tim Kennedy's 12-week training program called "Tactical Monster." If you are reading this guide and you feel like matriculation is too close to reach your goals in time, I don't want you to worry. You won't be the only one that didn't fully prepare. Remember the mentality from earlier in the guide: you aren't the only one struggling. Even if you come to VMI in peak physical condition, the ratline will not be easy. It takes its toll on everyone in its own, unique way. Come ready to work on your weaknesses and DO NOT be the person that avoids facing them. There's a lot more respect given to those who show up and try their hardest, than those who visibly give up and say, "I can't do this."

To be brutally honest, if you push off physical fitness, try to "milk" your injuries, or become known as the person that gives up easily, you won't earn any respect from your peers and that will follow you throughout your cadetship. That's the harsh truth. A big part of being a leader is having a physical presence and leading by example. If you can't pass the VFT, you certainly shouldn't be able to hold a leadership position, where you are expected to be a model cadet. Now, was I always a model cadet? No. No. No. I learned the most at VMI through my many mistakes, and while my intent is for this guide to save you from that pain, you are going to make mistakes too.

I want to apologize to those of you that hoped this section would consist of a bodybuilding program or Olympic weightlifting program. I could extend this guide for another twenty pages or more and talk about physical fitness until my hands fall off. However, you have to realize that nobody is going to care that a rat can bench press 225 pounds or more if they have absolutely zero endurance and fail the VFT. The time to "get big" is after the ratline, when you have more control over your schedule and what types of workouts you complete.

Nutrition

If you haven't figured it out by now, Crozet Hall isn't even slightly comparable to Virginia Tech's dining facilities. Ask any cadet, "how's the food?" More often than not, they will just laugh or say, "oh, you'll see." Comforting. I have good news. The food has gotten better in recent years. More on that soon…

At VMI, everyone has mandatory morning and evening formations called Breakfast Roll Call (BRC) and Supper Roll Call (SRC). From here, we march down to the mess hall (Crozet) and indulge in an all-you-can-eat buffet. Sounds great, right? Not exactly. You can accelerate your performance and success at VMI by paying attention to what you're putting in your body (Duh). But of course, this is a double-edged sword. You could be crushing it in the gym and working your body to death, and you see zero improvements. It all comes back to nutrition. My dykes often told me to "eat for function, not for pleasure." As extreme as this sounds, it holds a lot of truth. Your nutrition can even affect your academic performance. For example, everyone has experienced that post-thanksgiving meal exhaustion. It turns out that this exhaustion is because of the effect that consuming carbohydrates has on the amino acid content in your blood. Without getting too in-depth, here's a quick run-down of what happens: Carbohydrates stimulate the release of insulin, which removes all the amino acids from your blood except for tryptophan. Now tryptophan has nothing to compete with in order to cross the blood-brain barrier and enters the brain. Since it's a pre-cursor to serotonin and melatonin, you start to feel sleepy. Therefore, if I know that I have a big test to study for at night, I'm not going to eat a large helping of mashed potatoes and bread at SRC. Similarly, if my goal is to improve my run time, I'm not going to fill my stomach with fried foods, because they are rough on your stomach and overall digestion. Luckily, you don't have to become a nutritional wizard in order to figure these things out at VMI. Here are some general guidelines that I use and have found effective:

1. I don't drink soda or eat fried foods—unless it's a Friday and I want to reward myself for a successful week.

2. I get a big serving of spinach, broccoli, and a banana with almost every meal—this is a good way to ensure you are getting your greens and keeping your potassium levels up. I typically eat these first, that way if I get full at least I got the essential and healthy foods in my body.

3. I always eat breakfast—your body needs fuel in order to perform…why wouldn't you feed it after it has

been running on empty all night?

4. The quantity of food I consume is based on how much exercise I got or will be getting throughout that day: more exercise=more fuel, more fuel=better performance, better performance=better results, etc.

5. Sometimes I replace lunch with a big protein shake—this is a controversial one, but I discovered that if I eat a big breakfast and big supper, then I can use lunch hours to get more done and ultimately go to bed earlier at the end of the day.

These five practices are the things that have worked for me and might not work as well for others. Regardless, I would recommend at least giving them a shot and seeing if you receive the same results.

As I stated earlier, the quality of food that VMI serves has improved greatly in the last few years. When I was a rat, all you could get for lunch was chicken patties (processed fried chicken), pasta, and the sandwich/salad bar. The new company, Parkhurst, has greatly expanded the food options for cadets. We even have a great burrito/burrito bowl line that serves as a great way to get the carbs/protein you need. Don't get me wrong- the food won't get you excited and you won't say "oh, wow, yum" when consuming it, but it's better than it has been in the past.

Lastly, I want to stress water intake. You should drink at least two cups of water with every meal. Another thing that I think every cadet/rat should do is get a big water bottle and sip on it throughout the day. As a rat, you're going to sweat almost continuously. You need to keep up with your hydration to maximize your recovery and avoid cramping. Hydration will also help with a properly functioning brain, so don't neglect drinking water while studying.

SLEEP

Sleep is critical if you wish to be successful at VMI. Honestly, developing good sleep habits might be the hardest thing to do during your cadetship. The reason for this is that every year at VMI is so much different from the last. An even worse reality is that every week is so much different from the last. You can be slammed one week and have barely any work to do the following week. For this reason, you have to set strict guidelines for yourself and stick to them as closely as you can. Unfortunately, I really didn't figure this out until second class year (junior year). On top of my Vice President class duties, Master Sergeant duties, Army MS3 responsibilities, I was enrolled in some of my hardest chemistry courses with twenty-one credits. In the beginning, I tried to do what I did in years past and finish most of my work in the evening. After staying up until 0200 or 0300 almost every day for a few weeks, I noticed that I was destroying myself. I had zero energy, my mentality was awful, and I wasn't being my normal and outgoing self. People even noticed this change and would constantly ask me if I was okay or if something tragic happened in my life. All of this accumulated into my questioning why I was even at VMI in the first place, and asking myself, "Is this even worth it?" I was definitely at a low point.

After those few weeks, I realized the root of this huge issue. Sleep. I was averaging three to four hours of sleep a night. This was frustrating because it seemed like there were no ways to fix it. There was no way I was going to neglect my work; I would end up feeling equally as bad about myself if my grades dropped. This is where time management really came in. I had to utilize every minute of every day and strategically do my work slowly throughout each day. I could no longer save it all for the evening study hours. I made the decision that, no matter what, I was going to go to bed before midnight every night. This would allow me to get approximately six to seven hours a night. To see how I did this, go back to the time management section of the guide and reread it.

Let me tell you what, the results were incredible. Slowly, and I mean SLOWLY, I regained my energy and quality of life. Not only that, but my grades actually improved. Without sleep, your brain can't properly function, your muscles can't recover sufficiently, and you can't maintain a positive and motivated attitude. If you're planning on following my advice from the academics section of this guide, then you shouldn't have much to worry about as a rat. You shouldn't be overwhelmed by credits and should have more than enough time to be asleep by TAPS (2330) every night. The reason I'm stressing this section, however, is because you need to realize that after you breakout, you get your phone back and you will have many more responsibilities. You can't go back to the high school ways of getting into bed at a reasonable time and staying up on your phone for another one to two hours. It might not affect you immediately, but you will slowly experience the negative effects over time. Remember your priorities. You'll have time for social media on the weekends.

Leadership

While you might not see it at first, VMI has more leadership opportunities available than you could ever imagine. There's the honor system, regimental system (those cool guys that stand out front during parades and get to train the rats throughout the ratline), the class system (consisting of the General Committee, the Officer of the Guard Association, and the Cadet Equity Association), academic organizations (National Honors Societies and major-specific clubs), NCAA teams (team captains), club sports (Cadet in Charge, team captains), and even more. Perhaps the most underrated or overseen leadership position, however, is the dyke system. For those of you that don't know, a dyke is a first class cadet (senior) that is assigned to take care of one or two rats throughout the ratline. Your dyke will ultimately be your lifeline throughout your tough times at VMI. You can go to his/her room during authorized times during the day and he/she will counsel you and hopefully help you reach your goals. Each dyke-rat relationship is unique. For example, I knew my dyke before coming to VMI. Even though he wasn't the same major as me, didn't have military aspirations, and numerous other differences between us, he became my go-to person for help during the ratline and even to this day. Don't know anyone at VMI? Worried about finding a dyke? Don't be. The dyke committee will make sure that you're paired up with a great member of their class and will keep an eye on you if a change/swap needs to occur. Even if you don't acquire leadership positions throughout your cadetship, just know that YOU WILL have the best one of all when you become a first classman.

So how do I become a leader at VMI? This is a loaded question. My best advice is to just be yourself and constantly work on your weaknesses. By doing this, you will create a great resume and set yourself up for success once interviews begin. What if your grades aren't the best and you keep getting in trouble? There are STILL opportunities! While you might not be the best candidate for a "ranker's" position (Company Corporal, etc.), there are still class elections. For organizations such as the General Committee and the Honor Court, people are selected through a voting system within your class. An electronic ballot will be sent out to your entire class and whoever receives the most votes will be placed in those positions. As you progress through your cadetship, the General Committee will start interviewing members of their class for leadership positions on the Officer of the Guard Association and the Cadet Equity Association. While academic performance and physical fitness performance are still considered for these positions, they are much less important since your peers are the ones conducting the interviews. I won't get into what exactly each organization does, because you will learn more and more about these positions throughout the training you will receive during the ratline. The main point is just to understand that there are many different routes when it comes to leadership at VMI.

I will now go over two leadership qualities that I've seen success with during my time at VMI. Possibly the biggest one is leading by example. As a leader, your goal is to inspire and motivate your subordinates to succeed. Beyond that, your goal should be to provide them the advice and tools so that they can succeed, both as an individual and a team. The best way to do this is by supplementing your advice with action. If you tell a rat that they need to make sure their shave is up to standard every day, then you better be sure as hell that your shave is perfect as well. There is nothing worse than a hypocrite. Just like anyone else, if someone tells me to do something and I keep seeing them doing the complete opposite, I'm not going to do it either. As cliché as it sounds, practice what you preach.

The next leadership quality that took me a long time to discover is transparency. You could also group this quality with honesty. Whether you realize it or not, people want to know what is going on in the organization. If you are planning on implementing a big change, then you should involve people in the process so that you can get feedback or even better ideas. As a leader, we always want to think that we have the answer to any problem and that it's our sole responsibility to come up with a solution. I learned quickly that this is blatant ignorance. If you take the time to sit down with people and explain the situation or problem, you will be pleasantly surprised to see that they want to help.

What can you do as a rat? While you won't be in any leadership positions, you can still start forming good habits. Probably the most important habit to implement is being a good BR. By developing a sense of what we call "brother rat spirit," you will feel invested in the ratline and feel better about yourself overall. If you see one of your BR's having a rough day, take time to sit down with them and ask them how they're doing. Maybe they had a family member pass away, failed a test that morning, didn't pass a fitness test, or are questioning their decision to come to VMI. Whatever their struggle is, make it your mission to lift their spirit and offer any help that you can provide. This is the beauty of VMI and the main reason why the alumni network is so strong after graduation. By just being a good human being and extending a helping hand to those that are struggling, you are a leader. You might not hold a fancy title or get any recognition, but you are shaping your mentality to be a successful leader by putting others first. People will feed off your energy and when it comes to a time when you might be struggling, they will recognize that and feel compelled to help. After all, VMI is one big family and it is impossible to get through it alone.

While this section could turn into something much longer, I want to close it out so that this guide doesn't become overwhelming for someone with a busy schedule. The last thing I'll say is that there's no golden roadmap to leadership success. Every person runs into their own challenges and experiences throughout their time at VMI. While the goal is to always do the right thing and act in a timely manner, I've probably learned the most through failure. You'll always remember the failures because of the frustration and disappointment that accompanied them. It's up to you to evaluate what you did wrong and learn from it. By doing so, you will continue to fine tune your leadership style and eliminate weaknesses as you progress. You will fail on a daily basis at VMI. Learn to embrace it and look at it with a different perspective. Those are the experiences that you will fall back on constantly throughout your cadetship and even throughout the rest of your life.

Finding the Balance

If you've made it this far in my guide, then you've been hit with a lot of information and advice. I realized that if I ended the guide after my leadership section, I wouldn't even know where to begin or what to do if I were heading to VMI for the first time. So, if you're having that feeling, know that it's a normal reaction. You're about to embark on a long, arduous path that will test you in ways that you never thought possible. I still have hard days. I still make a lot of mistakes. As my mother always says, we are our worst critics. You have to know when to give yourself a break, or when to step back and take a deep breath. It's okay to treat yourself to a soda and some fried food, to go out with your BR's for a couple drinks, or to occasionally put off some work because you are having an awful day. This is one of the realizations that I think some guides fail to address. You have to slowly develop these habits and realize that none of them will be easy. All you can do is have a positive mindset, rely on your BR's, remember why you're here, and continue to make adjustments and evaluate the results. Congratulations on taking the first step towards your success at VMI. Just by reading this, you are displaying your strong desire to get the most out of VMI. You're one step ahead of countless people that have entered the system before you, and I have no doubt that you're going to come out of VMI one step ahead of those people as well. I strongly encourage you to remember the things I've said in this guide and refer back to it whenever you are having a rough time. Thank you for reading and welcome to the family.

Colin D. Smith

Acknowledgments

I have to start by thanking my amazing mom and dad, Jay and Erica. From supporting my decision to go to VMI and pursue an Army career to helping me push through my hardest points in life, I'm extremely grateful for everything you've done for me. Tyler and I are lucky to have such great people to look up to and learn from, and I have no doubt that the foundation you laid early in my life has been the backbone for everything I've learned to this point.

Thank you to my brother, SGT Tyler Smith '17. Without your decision to go to Benedictine College Preparatory and then the Virginia Military Institute, I would have never made it to where I am today. By getting deployed mid-school-year and having the strength to come back to VMI to finish, you possess the most persistent and hardworking qualities that will carry you far in life. Thank you for setting an amazing example and always keeping me in check.

I would like to thank my beautiful grandparents, Movane & Dennis Smith, and Diane O'Connell. Mommo, I can't thank you enough for being such a professional, loving, and strong woman. You embody the word success and motivate me to be a man of God each and every day. Granddad, I miss you dearly and you're a huge part of why I chose to pursue a military career. You were so knowledgeable and successful and I can only hope to be half the husband, father, and grandfather that you were. Thank you for looking out for me each and every day of my life. Grandma, thank you for being such a loving and kind individual. You never fail to support me in all of my endeavors. Raising three amazing kids as a single parent is no small feat and you are a shining representation of the adage "anything is possible."

To my roommates, Kyle Coons & Henry Cascella. You've seen it all. VMI gave me my two best friends and I'm excited to watch you grow and succeed in your Army careers. I can't thank you guys enough for having my back no matter what, and having the strength to tell me when I was jacked up.

I want to thank my incredible dykes, Matthew Armentrout '16, 1LT Dillon Wright '16, 1LT Nick Nadeau '16, 1LT Christian Rowcliffe '16, and 1LT Phil Morton '16. I couldn't have asked for better role models and mentors. You guys were the ultimate display of brotherhood and a lot of the things I covered in this book were lessons that I learned from you. Thank you for showing us the profound impact that dykes can have on rats at VMI.

To LTC Kevin Faust '96, I want to thank you for providing me guidance during my cadetship. You helped me overcome the lowest point of my life. You dropped everything just to be the person I needed at the time. For that, I'm forever in your debt and this book would have never been possible without you.

I'd like to thank MAJ Brandon Lindsey '02. I don't know how you came back to VMI to be an Army ROTC instructor this year (or if you even had a choice), but I'm grateful that you did. You have shown me that my outgoing personality is still compatible with the Army and that people always come first.

Lastly, thank you Tyler Davidson. It was crushing to have my best friend pass away during high school, but you taught me so much about myself. Your death served as a pivotal moment in my life and I know you've been looking out for me ever since. Love you brother.

Made in the USA
Middletown, DE
23 December 2021